ALSO BY ERIC MAISEL

FICTION

The Black Narc

The Kingston Papers

Dismay

The Blackbirds of Mulhouse

The Fretful Dancer

NONFICTION

Van Gogh's Blues

20 Communication Tips at Work

Sleep Thinking

The Creativity Book

Deep Writing

Staying Sane in the Arts

Artists Speak

A Life in the Arts

Fearless Creating

Affirmations for Artists

Fearless Presenting

Living the Writer's Life

20 Communication Tips for Families

JEREMY P. TARCHER • PUTNAM

A MEMBER OF

PENGUIN PUTNAM INC.

NEW YORK

299 Things
Writers Should
Never Say
to Themselves

Write

Mind

Eric Maisel

(And What
They Should
Say Instead)

Most Tarcher/Putnam books are available at special quantity
discounts for bulk purchase for sales promotions, premiums, fund-raising,
and educational needs. Special books or book excerpts also can be created to
fit specific needs. For details, write Putnam Special Markets,
375 Hudson Street, New York, NY 10014.

JEREMY P. TARCHER/PUTNAM
a member of
Penguin Putnam Inc.
375 Hudson Street
New York, NY 10014
www.penguinputnam.com

Library of Congress Cataloging-in-Publication Data

Maisel, Eric, date.
Write mind : 299 things writers should never say to themselves,
and what they should say instead / Eric Maisel.

p.   cm.
ISBN 1-58542-136-7
1. Authorship—Psychological aspects.   2. Authorship.   I. Title: Write mind,
two hundred ninety-nine things writers should never say to themselves,
and what they should say instead.   II. Title.

PN171.P83 M355   2002   2001046310
808'.02'019—dc21

Printed in the United States of America
1   3   5   7   9   10   8   6   4   2

This book is printed on acid-free paper. ∞

BOOK DESIGN BY DEBORAH KERNER/DANCING BEARS DESIGN

FOR ANN,

25 YEARS INTO THIS ADVENTURE

INTRODUCTION

The central premise of cognitive therapy is that wrong thinking causes much of the pain and suffering we experience. The Roman Epictetus put it this way: "Do not surrender your mind." Wise men and wise women have informed us since the dawn of our species that we are what we think. In this book I want to help you think right as a writer by presenting you with 299 wrong things that writers say to themselves and the things they ought to be saying instead.

Wrong thinking produces pain and suffering. Wrong thinking is also very common, even ubiquitous. Therefore, one solution to the problem of pain and suffering is not to think at all. Indeed, this is the solution adopted by many human beings. They throw out the baby with the bathwater by living in the restricted silence of "No hard-to-manage thoughts for me!" One unfortunate result of this decision is to banish their creativity to another country.

This helps explain what at first glance seems paradoxical—that thoughtful people have more trouble with their thoughts than do unthoughtful people. If you choose to think but you aren't able to distinguish wrong thinking from right thinking, then you experience more pain and suffering than you would if you didn't think at all. However, the answer isn't refusing to think. The answer is learning to distinguish right thinking from wrong thinking.

This also means understanding that entertaining dreams can cause pain. Desire can cause pain. Craving justice can cause pain. Everything good, valuable, and laudable can become a source of pain once the mind wants it. Again, the answer isn't not to want these things! The answer is to be alert to the fact that pain may be coming and to know what to say in response to a wrong thought.

Let me clarify what I'm saying with a hypothetical example.

You have a book published and in its third year it sells only 500 copies. In the fourth it sells half that number. One day you receive a letter from your editor informing you that your book is being put out of print. Why should this news make you suffer? Few copies were selling.

Surely you saw the handwriting on the wall. If you like, you can attempt to sell the book to another publisher, one who may do a stronger job of marketing it. Or you can make the text available as an e-book. In short, there is nothing surprising about this news and it may even be an opportunity in the life of your book.

Still, virtually every writer will react to this news with great pain. The pain is in the self-talk and in the way the writer interprets the meaning of this event. One writer will say, "I used to be a published author; now I am nothing." Another writer will say, "I pinned so much hope on this book and now all hope is gone." A third writer will say, "Now that I've completely failed with this book, no one will ever want to publish me." A fourth writer will say, "This book was good and deserved better marketing, better promotion, a better cover, better everything. I have been treated unfairly." A fifth writer will say another pain-inducing comment, a sixth will say another, and so on.

All of this pain is caused by the mind. The facts are that the book is not selling well, for whatever reasons, and that the publisher will put it out of print. A writer can look at this as a normal occurrence, an opportunity, or a calamity. He can say, "They put it out of its misery like a dog!" or ask, "What is the next step in the life of this book?" If he holds this event as the equivalent of the death of a child or another unbearable pain, he has transformed a minor moment in his long career as a writer into a horror, a humiliation, an enormous defeat.

The Buddha said, "Get a grip on your mind!" As a thoughtful person, you have the ability to challenge your thoughts that bring you pain or that cause you not to write. What you also need are the understanding and the will. If you have the understanding and the will, then when a wrong thought pops into your head you will see it clearly for what it is, the product of some doubt, fear, reluctance, or inner conflict.

This is the first step, clearly hearing the thought and recognizing it for what it is. The next step is saying, "I don't want this thought!" In cognitive therapy, this is called *thought confrontation*. Without hesitation and without embarrassment, you say "No!" The final step is to replace the unbidden, unfortunate thought with a right thought. In cognitive therapy, this is called *thought substitution*.

With the right thought in place, the pain ends.

At a recent writers' conference a writer asked me, "Can I really do that? Can I get rid of thoughts I've been thinking my whole life and replace them with new ones?" I replied, "If you want to." That is the complete answer. You may not want to because you have suffered too much pain and can't stand the idea of more rejection or more criticism. You may not want to because you have an ingrained belief that you have nothing to say. You may not want to for one or another of a hundred different reasons. In that case, you won't.

You will keep your current thoughts and all the pain and suffering they engender. Yes, change is deep work, because you must go down and wrestle with long-standing beliefs and serious doubts. Still, that is what you want to do. Isn't that so? Just begin and, who knows, maybe the work will be easier than you imagine, for change can also happen effortlessly, in an instant. Maybe you are primed right now for that miracle. Isn't that possible?

The goal of this work is not to produce a detached monk. Few people become an empty vessel, able to take everything in stride, able to take every defeat, every insult, every rejection, the destruction of their families, their own deaths, and everything else under the sun in a purely philosophical and detached way. But even if one could arrive at that place, that is not the goal. We should experience pain and suffering, because that means that we care and that we intend to matter. It is that other portion of pain and suffering that we want to eliminate—the unnecessary portion that the mind makes for no good reason.

Nor is the goal of this work to become a Pollyanna. You do not replace wrong thoughts with happy thoughts. You replace them with affirmative thoughts, which, however, are full of true understanding and an appreciation of reality. You do not replace "I can never write my novel" with "If I sing a happy tune, I can write my novel in three days flat!" You do not replace "No one will publish my collection of poems" with "Everyone will want to publish my collection of poems!" You replace the first with "I can write my novel" and the second with "I will do a terrific job marketing my collection—the best job I can possibly do."

Right mind is not happy mind and where it leads is to work, not to ease.

Is the sort of cognitive change I'm suggesting possible? Many clinicians would say no. They'd argue that unconscious motives, basic instincts, beliefs calcified in childhood, and other mechanisms out of the conscious control of the individual produce most, if not all, thought. They'd say, "Look at severe depression. Look at obsessive thinking. Look at intractable behavior disorders, anxiety syndromes, addictions. It is not at *all* easy for people to change their minds!" My reply to the psychodynamic view is that I neither agree nor disagree. There is evidence to support the idea that you think your thoughts and evidence to support the idea that your thoughts think you.

A piece of interesting counterevidence to the psychodynamic view is that psychotic individuals—that is, folks presumably least in control of their thoughts—are often able to hold a perfectly rational conversation if it suits them to do so. If, say, you offer them the chance to move from the locked ward to the unlocked ward and that move interests them, they will do a beautiful job of making a case for the switch. This is not final proof that we are in better charge of our thoughts than we might believe, just a reminder that we do not really know one way or the other.

None of this is to imply that we will do a perfect job of preventing wrong thinking from infiltrating our consciousnesses, noticing it when it occurs, or instantly introducing right thinking to counteract our wrong thoughts. But we can get much better at all three. I train creativity coaches and we discuss these issues. One creativity coach-in-training shared the following anecdote. This is an excellent, and I hope inspiring, example of how far we can come.

"This week, I caught myself in a thought that surprised me. I'm sitting on my bed with a drawing pad across my lap, charting chunks of my novel. Five or six large pages, vivid with ovals and arrows, spill across the bed and onto the floor. For weeks I'd been feeling pleased that my current mix of characters and events had attracted a strong flow, especially since not having enough material had been an old fear. I'd been lucky to strike a gusher. So who is this saying, 'You know how you overcomplicate things. Keep it simple, can't you?'

"I didn't notice this commentary at first. I'd been intent on what I was doing and believed I was enjoying the process when I started to feel a dark mood, rather like what happens in a science-fiction movie when an alien spaceship casts a giant shadow over a city. I wanted to shoo it away. Then I finally noticed the words I'd been hearing. I've had lots of experience at counteracting blurts, so I didn't stop to analyze. Instantly, I treated myself to a positive affirmation and printed it at the top of the page I'd been working on. Right-mind: 'You have wonderfully rich resources to draw upon.' The spaceship withdrew and I happily filled another eight or so pages, printing the positive thought at the top of each page."

My hope is that you can learn to think right. I hope you can learn to say, "I am writing today" instead of, "I am so tired." I hope you can learn to say, "I wrote an awful first novel and now I'm starting on my second novel" instead of, "I wrote an awful first novel and that proves I'm an idiot."

Neither you nor I can answer any of the ultimate questions. But don't you feel a little confident that you can substitute a right thought for a wrong thought? If you are not sure one way or the other, take yes for an answer. If you're convinced that the answer is no, opt for yes anyway. Unless you say yes to the possibility that you can change your mind, and with it your life, you will have said no with a vengeance.

I've taken the liberty of letting in a little humor here and there. The book's title is a pun, and the notion of "wrong" things that we say to ourselves and "right" things that we should substitute would be an overly authoritarian message if it weren't offered a little tongue-in-cheek. But of course my basic message is a serious one. You want to write more often and more deeply; you want to create some beautiful things. To meet these goals, you must improve how you communicate with yourself and strive to acquire a right mind or a better mind—or, to be a little light-hearted about it, a "write mind."

Sometimes you feel that everything in the world, from your friends to your outlook, from your culture to your day job, conspire to prevent you from writing. You also know that your worst enemy is you, and whether you call it your personality, your mind-set, your neurosis, your weakness, your fright, or something else, it is still you. It is hard to take the fact that you are the problem, and there is nothing very humorous about that. But I am offering you a path to freedom: right thinking.

How will you use this book? My hope is that its message and its lessons will seep into your consciousness and, perhaps for the first time, you will begin to notice the wrong-headed things you say to yourself. You will begin to have the experience of stepping back from your thoughts and saying, "Wow, what did I just think? What ever was that thought for?"

At first you may not know what to do next, but eventually you will find yourself disputing your wrong thinking and experimenting with new thoughts, most of which will be better than your self-defeating thoughts and some of which will be really right. Slowly but surely you will change your inner landscape, the way you speak to yourself, and your life.

Write
Mind

1.

WRONG MIND: "I am a stupid, neurotic person with no real talent. I don't really matter."

RIGHT MIND: "I matter."

2.

WRONG MIND: "I worry about virtually everything."

RIGHT MIND: "I wonder about virtually everything."

3.

WRONG MIND: "Maybe, maybe, maybe, maybe, maybe, maybe."

RIGHT MIND: "Yes."

4.

WRONG MIND: "In some important sense, I am ruined."

RIGHT MIND: "Many wounded people have written. I can be a wounded writer. Maybe I can even become a healed writer."

5.

WRONG MIND: "It is much too late to start."

RIGHT MIND: "I can have my novel written in a year or two."

6.

WRONG MIND: "There is far too much going on in my life for me to write."

RIGHT MIND: "I will write first thing every morning."

7.

WRONG MIND: "My to-do list is so full that there is no room on it for writing."

RIGHT MIND: "Writing is at the top of my to-do list."

8.

WRONG MIND: "My mind is so noisy that I can't think straight."

RIGHT MIND: "I can quiet my mind just by saying, 'Hush.'"

9.

WRONG MIND: "I hate mistakes and messes."
RIGHT MIND: "I am easy with mistakes and messes."

"Whatever you think,
be sure it is what you think."

T. S. ELIOT

10.

WRONG MIND: "I hope people will understand what I'm intending to say in this piece."
RIGHT MIND: "I hope *some* people will understand what I'm intending to say in this piece."

11.

WRONG MIND: "I need what I am writing to be loved."

RIGHT MIND: "I need what I am writing to be strong."

12.

WRONG MIND: "Since I can't possibly make a living from writing, there is no reason to write."

RIGHT MIND: "I write to find out."

13.

WRONG MIND: "Somebody has the answer and if I take enough writing workshops I am sure to happen upon the answer."

RIGHT MIND: "I learn to write by writing and I learn to market by marketing."

14.

WRONG MIND: "Editors and agents scare me."

RIGHT MIND: "I get anxious, but I can also be professional."

15.

WRONG MIND: "Maybe an editor won't notice that my nonfiction book proposal isn't very strong."

RIGHT MIND: "I am going to work *very* hard on my proposal and make it letter perfect."

Right Silence

You are trying to write a novel but you haven't worked on it for months. You are thinking that maybe you will attend a workshop, hire a freelance editor, change the novel's point of view, or abandon the novel altogether. Instead of entertaining these thoughts, say, "I need the courage to sit still; I need to quiet my mind; I need to enter right silence."

You get to right silence by affirming each step of the journey to right silence. Say the following things—and do them.

"I can sit still."

"I can sit still and be with my anxiety."

"I can sit still and begin to quiet my noisy mind."

"I can sit quietly."

"I can sit quietly."

"I can sit quietly and begin to engage with my novel."

"I can sit quietly, begin to engage with my novel, and shut out the noise that wells up again."

"I can be with my novel in right silence."

Choose to be one of the rare ones who practices inviting, honoring, embracing, and affirming silence. Say, "I know it is hard, but I can achieve right silence." Affirm yourself through courageous lifelong practice.

16.

WRONG MIND: "I would love to write."

RIGHT MIND: "I intend to write."

17.

WRONG MIND: "I have to make sure never to reveal who I am in my writing or else people will see that I am a monster."

RIGHT MIND: "I am willing to reveal myself."

18.

WRONG MIND: "I have nothing to say."

RIGHT MIND: "If I write truthfully and carefully, it may turn out that I have something to say."

19.

WRONG MIND: "I am a genius and agents and editors are idiots."

RIGHT MIND: "It does me no good to inflate myself or to deflate others. My job is to write well and to sell my wares."

20.

WRONG MIND: "I am a genius and writers who write bestsellers are idiots."

RIGHT MIND: "It does me no good to inflate myself or to deflate others. My job is to write well and to sell my wares."

21.

WRONG MIND: "I can't write because I won't be able to tolerate all the rejections."

RIGHT MIND: "Not writing is the bigger rejection: the rejection of my own voice."

22.

WRONG MIND: "No, no, no, no, no, no, no."

RIGHT MIND: "Yes."

23.

WRONG MIND: "I can't choose what to write."

RIGHT MIND: "I can choose what to write."

"Silence is
the cornerstone of character."

CHARLES ALEXANDER EASTMAN

24.

WRONG MIND: "Freud was right when he said that writer's block is simply self-censorship. I can't write because I am always censoring myself."

RIGHT MIND: "I will write even though I am a little ashamed of myself."

25.

WRONG MIND: "I can't write when the temperature is below sixty-eight degrees or above seventy-two degrees."

RIGHT MIND: "I can write in a thunderstorm by the light of lightning bolts."

26.

WRONG MIND: "Writers write; publishers sell."

RIGHT MIND: "Writers write; writers sell."

27.

WRONG MIND: "I would secretly like to kidnap and torture a literary agent."

RIGHT MIND: "Literary agents represent projects that they think they can sell. Nothing could be less mysterious or more impersonal."

28.

WRONG MIND: "I don't know what my novel is about."

RIGHT MIND: "I don't need to know what my novel is about in order to write it. All I need is a nub of an idea and courage."

29.

WRONG MIND: "Everybody says I should be a writer."

RIGHT MIND: "I say I should be a writer."

30.

WRONG MIND: "Most of the time the so-called experts are frauds or fools, so the fact that I am no expert shouldn't prevent an editor from publishing my nonfiction book."

RIGHT MIND: "I need credentials if I am going to publish nonfiction. If mine aren't adequate, I have to figure out how to beef them up."

31.

WRONG MIND: "I will definitely get back to my novel next week."

RIGHT MIND: "Ready or not, I am heading to the computer."

32.

WRONG MIND: "I never seem to have ideas. I must be a dull, unimaginative person."

RIGHT MIND: "Of course I have ideas."

Snow Globe

When you shake up a snow globe, first the snow swirls chaotically, then it begins to settle nicely, and then all is quiet again. When you think about writing, you do something equivalent to that shaking. You shake yourself up and make inner chaos and worry. Experiencing all that chaos and worry, you don't want to write. What you forget is that you could settle down and achieve necessary quiet, if only you gave yourself half a chance.

Picture a snow globe whenever thinking about writing shakes you up. Picture the chaos, then the settling, then the quiet. When things are swirling around you or swirling inside of you, use the image of a snow globe to help yourself settle down, get quiet, and write.

33.

WRONG MIND: "It is who you know that determines whether you will succeed as a writer."

RIGHT MIND: "I am willing and able to network."

34.

WRONG MIND: "I have written so little over the years, I must have nothing to say."

RIGHT MIND: "I am ready to write in a steady, everyday way and put the past behind me."

35.

WRONG MIND: "I am much stupider than I like to admit. Therefore I can only write stupid things."

RIGHT MIND: "Sometimes I write beautifully and brilliantly. Therefore it must be true that beautiful and brilliant things are inside of me."

36.

WRONG MIND: "I can't write if I outline. Outlining kills the creative spark in me."

RIGHT MIND: "I can write with an outline and I can write without an outline. I can even write in the shower with a bar of soap."

37.

WRONG MIND: "I can't write *without* an outline. If I don't have an outline I meander all over the place and end up in Bulgaria."

RIGHT MIND: "I can write with an outline and I can write without an outline. I can even write standing on my head, until I pass out."

38.

WRONG MIND: "For some people, writing is easy, but for me it is very hard. Therefore, I must not be a writer."

RIGHT MIND: "Sometimes writing is easy and sometimes writing is hard. So sometimes I will have it easy and sometimes I will have it hard."

39.

WRONG MIND: "I am much too special to have to revise what I write. Hack writers revise and gifted writers like me don't need to bother."

RIGHT MIND: "There is very often the glimmer of something excellent in my drafts, but it takes work and more work to get the stone to finally shine."

40.

WRONG MIND: "There is no market for what I write."

RIGHT MIND: "I will try every trick in the book to get my wares to market. I will try presses that put out three books a year and presses that put out only two. Not until I try one thousand and three tricks will I conclude that there is no market for what I write."

41.

WRONG MIND: "My second novel sold more poorly than my first novel and my third novel sold more poorly than my second novel. I am sinking into oblivion and no editor will ever love me again."

RIGHT MIND: "That I have published three novels is ultimately a significant plus and I will make my fourth novel as strong and good as I can make it."

42.

WRONG MIND: "Since I am virtually a mental wreck, how can I be expected to write?"

RIGHT MIND: "I do need to take care of my mental health, but maybe writing is part of the way I can help myself do exactly that."

43.

WRONG MIND: "What I want to write about is too painful to contemplate. Therefore, I won't write."

RIGHT MIND: "I have two choices, to write about painful things, which might even be therapeutic, or else to write about other things. The only choice I don't have is not to write."

44.

WRONG MIND: "Jane is a wonderful writer. When I read what she's written, I want to kill myself."

RIGHT MIND: "I love good writing and I refuse to start hating it just because I am sad and disappointed about my career."

45.

WRONG MIND: "Jane has an unfair advantage. She is part Plutonian and nobody but Plutonians get published today."

RIGHT MIND: "If I put on a wig and use a nom de plume, I might pass for Plutonian. Seriously, there are always advantages and disadvantages in life. What I have to focus on is doing excellent work."

46.

WRONG MIND: "Jane is a lucky writer. She has a husband who supports her and who doesn't call her a parasite. I want to kill Jane."

RIGHT MIND: "I will not let envy define me, derail me, or destroy me."

47.

WRONG MIND: "Jane is such a self-promoter! Whenever I see her name in the newspaper I want to burn down her house."

RIGHT MIND: "I am okay with the idea that, just like Jane, I must promote myself."

48.

WRONG MIND: "I seem to be thinking about Jane again. She is my nemesis!"

RIGHT MIND: "As long as I am thinking about Jane, I'm not thinking about my writing. Now really, self, which should I be thinking about?"

Ego

A concert violinist once came to see me for counseling, complaining bitterly about how she hated turning the pages of musical scores during performances. Why? Because she had to turn the pages for herself *and her seat mate*. He was higher ranking, she was lower ranking. She had to stop everything to turn the pages and he didn't have to lift a finger. That rankled to the extent that she wanted to kill him.

"I hate turning the pages!" is wrong mind. It is insatiable ego—"greedy mind," Buddhists call it—making an enormous amount of unnecessary pain and suffering. Right mind is "I am playing in a symphony orchestra! I am doing something I love! I am being paid to do it!"

49.

WRONG MIND: "I'm too big a coward to put my thoughts on paper. What if people hate what I write?"

RIGHT MIND: "I want to feel courageous and that means daring to write."

50.

WRONG MIND: "I can't write because if I completed something I'd be forced to try to sell it. That thought frightens me half to death."

RIGHT MIND: "I can learn to sell. Maybe I can even learn to sell without it feeling so scary. That being the case, it's time to write."

51.

WRONG MIND: "One hundred fifty-three editors have rejected my novel, which I know is just as good as the novels I read. Therefore, I will never write again."

RIGHT MIND: "I will write many novels, some of which will be published."

52.

WRONG MIND: "A hundred thousand authors are off writing romances. How can I compete against such numbers?"

RIGHT MIND: "I want to write an excellent romance. For now, my only goal is excellence."

53.

WRONG MIND: "That agent yawned when I pitched my project! I could have killed her!"

RIGHT MIND: "I'm not presenting my project well if it gets yawns. I need a better pitch."

54.

WRONG MIND: "I've been working in my field for fifteen years. Surely I have a nonfiction book to write."

RIGHT MIND: "I've been working in my field for fifteen years. I should think about what I've learned and see if I can organize my thoughts in a logical, systematic way."

55.

WRONG MIND: "I'd love to write a memoir, but then everyone in my family would despise me."

RIGHT MIND: "Telling the truth feels very important, but so does sparing feelings. Maybe a novel would be a better idea than a memoir. But before I make that choice, I should get some of my experiences down on paper and see what I'm actually talking about."

"Men are tormented by the opinions
they have of things,
not by the things themselves."

•

MICHEL DE MONTAIGNE

56.

WRONG MIND: "At the rate I'm going, I'll have twelve short stories written by the time I'm ninety."

RIGHT MIND: "I want to increase my output and I'm going to institute a new writing routine and a new writing regimen."

57.

WRONG MIND: "I want to write a mother-daughter novel, but I feel so guilty about the way I raised my daughter that whenever I think about that material I hate myself."

RIGHT MIND: "I am going to write a mother-daughter novel, not to undo the past, not to whitewash myself, and not as a substitute for mothering, but because that novel is so much in my heart to write."

58.

WRONG MIND: "I can't write in California. I need to be in New York."

RIGHT MIND: "I can write in California."

59.

WRONG MIND: "I can't write in my house. The dog next door is always barking."

RIGHT MIND: "I can write in my house."

60.

WRONG MIND: "I can't write at my computer. It hums too loudly."

RIGHT MIND: "I can write at my computer."

Distraction

I once gave a talk to a group of writers. We had convened in a restaurant and an oblivious waiter, crossing back and forth behind me as I spoke, accidentally unhooked my microphone on three different occasions. I could almost have paid him to do that, into such a grand tizzy did it send the audience.

"Can't you please STOP that!" they cried at him, the loudest when it happened the third time. But I waved my hand. "Hold on! There's no problem. I'm not upset and *I'm* the one who has to keep talking!"

What is a distraction? *Where* is distraction? No writer has ever done away with anxiety. No writer has ever escaped. Therefore, the potential for distraction is always with us, but it is up to us to be distracted or not to be distracted. If we are distracted, the biscuits burn. If we are distracted, we miss our stop. If we are distracted, we hop up from our writing. Then we are lost, without biscuits, not writing.

61.

WRONG MIND: "Everybody tells me that Mary is the only agent to work with, but she turned my proposal down. I guess I can't send it out anymore."

RIGHT MIND: "Mary rejected my proposal and that hurt. Now I need to send the proposal out again—and again, and again—and bravely risk more rejection."

62.

WRONG MIND: "My editor at Very Big Publishing changed virtually every word of my manuscript. I am going to send her chocolates with poison centers."

RIGHT MIND: "My editor at Very Big Publishing changed virtually every word of my manuscript, which hurt my feelings a lot. But her editing has made the book much better. I should thank her."

63.

WRONG MIND: "One agent told me one thing and another agent told me another thing. I guess they cancel each other out!"

RIGHT MIND: "Agents are taking the time to provide me with feedback on my proposal, which makes me feel good and convinces me that something is here. But I'm also hearing that more work is needed."

64.

WRONG MIND: "Reading four hundred novels would probably help me find my voice."

RIGHT MIND: "I will only find my voice by writing many novels, including the bad ones I will probably have to write, and learning by writing."

65.

WRONG MIND: "I hate the short story I've been trying to write so damned much."

RIGHT MIND: "I don't hate my story. I'm just sad that it's not all that I hoped it would be and that I haven't worked very well on it. I still love what it's about and I will try again."

66.

WRONG MIND: "I'm frightened of the short story I've been trying to write. It scares me just to think about it!"

RIGHT MIND: "I'm not scared of the short story. I'm just afraid that I'll make a mess and disappoint myself. I still love what the story's about and I will try again."

67.

WRONG MIND: "I am a shallow person, as evidenced by the shallow things I write."

RIGHT MIND: "Sometimes I'm shallow and sometimes I'm deep. The only question that concerns me is: How can I go deep more often?"

68.

WRONG MIND: "Finally I got something other than a form-letter rejection from an editor. But all she said was, 'I like this a lot but the pacing is off. It needs to be tighter and to start faster. Show it to me again when you've reworked it.' Well, my novel starts out just fine the way it is. As if I'd give her a second chance to read it!"

RIGHT MIND: "I'm going to get my novel tighter and faster over the next four weeks or die trying. Maybe this editor will hate my rewrite or maybe she will love it. At any rate, this is not an editorial response I am going to choose to ignore."

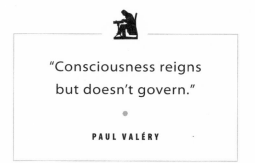

"Consciousness reigns
but doesn't govern."

PAUL VALÉRY

69.

WRONG MIND: "I've always been told that I'm not creative. Therefore I must not be."

RIGHT MIND: "I am at least as creative as the next person."

70.

WRONG MIND: "I've always been told to be nice. I'm not sure that nice girls should write."

RIGHT MIND: "I am not that nice and I'll write what I damn well please."

71.

WRONG MIND: "I've always been told to defer to others. I'm not sure that writing is a very deferential thing to do."

RIGHT MIND: "It's my turn."

72.

WRONG MIND: "I've been sitting here for fifteen minutes without writing a thing. I need a break!"

RIGHT MIND: "I've been sitting here for fifteen minutes without writing a thing and my anxiety is mounting. I need to quiet my nerves by doing a little deep breathing and by reciting my writing affirmations."

73.

WRONG MIND: "My horoscope says that I shouldn't write today."

RIGHT MIND: "The next chapter of my novel scares me and I'm looking for ways to avoid tackling it, but I'm going to write today anyway, even though I'm scared."

74.

WRONG MIND: "I have to bake pies for the church meeting, so I shouldn't write today."

RIGHT MIND: "The next chapter of my novel scares me and I'm looking for ways to avoid tackling it, but

I'm going to write today anyway, even though I'm scared."

75.

WRONG MIND: "I have to gather up all of our old clothes to give to Goodwill, so I shouldn't write today."

RIGHT MIND: "The next chapter of my novel scares me and I'm looking for ways to avoid tackling it, but I'm going to write today anyway, even though I'm scared."

Here Is the Anxiety. Where Is the Danger?

Anxiety is a signal of danger. It's a train whistle, but no train may be coming. Some evil spirit may have decided to pull the whistle, even though there is no danger. But because we hate the experience of anxiety, as soon as we hear the whistle we react by whistling louder, to drown out the signal.

We run to a cafe. We turn up the music. We open a bottle. We pick a fight. We certainly do not write.

We run because we fear the anxiety.

We leap off a bridge to avoid the buzzing of a bee.
We ought to stay put instead.

76.

WRONG MIND: "I can only write nonfiction. I'm not creative enough to write fiction."

RIGHT MIND: "I can write anything."

77.

WRONG MIND: "I can only write fiction. Nonfiction bores me and demands too much organization."

RIGHT MIND: "I can write anything."

78.

WRONG MIND: "I can only write poetry. Novels take too long."

RIGHT MIND: "I can write anything."

79.

WRONG MIND: "I can only write novels. Poetry requires some skill set that I don't possess."

RIGHT MIND: "I can write anything."

80.

WRONG MIND: "I need a master's in creative writing in order to impress agents and editors."

RIGHT MIND: "I need to write."

81.

WRONG MIND: "I can't write because I'm always worried about money."

RIGHT MIND: "My money worries are very real and they make me feel horrible. I hate my day job and I must do something about that. But I am going to carve out one hour a day when I refuse to think about money. During that hour I will let myself write without badgering myself about my financial situation."

82.

WRONG MIND: "I need to read another book on writing."

RIGHT MIND: "I need to write."

83.

WRONG MIND: "A trillion books are published each year. What chance do I have against those odds?"

RIGHT MIND: "A trillion books are published each year. There are so many opportunities for books to be published!"

84.

WRONG MIND: "Maybe I could publish with a small press, but that would feel like such a failure."

RIGHT MIND: "Small presses have their bestsellers and big presses have their bombs. I will not judge a press by its size."

85.

WRONG MIND: "Maybe I could self-publish, but that would feel like such a failure."

RIGHT MIND: "Self-publishing is no disgrace and sometimes it's exactly the right answer. Self-publishing is an option."

86.

WRONG MIND: "I wish that my novel were already written."

RIGHT MIND: "I am looking forward to the experience of writing my novel."

87.

WRONG MIND: "I wish that someone else would write my novel."

RIGHT MIND: "I am looking forward to the experience of writing my novel."

88.

WRONG MIND: "I'd like to do some writing but I should find a good copy editor first. That would help with my lousy grammar and punctuation. With a good copy editor aboard, I could write my book."

RIGHT MIND: "I'm scared about writing my book. Probably the best thing to do is to try to write it."

89.

WRONG MIND: "I'd like to do some writing but I should find a writers' group first. That support and feedback would really help me."

RIGHT MIND: "Some writers' groups are great, some writers' groups are mediocre, and some writers' groups are hellish. I guess I could check some out and see if I can find a good one. But I better not put off writing until I find the right group!"

A Too-Quiet Mind

Many people are plagued by what they think of as a too-quiet mind. They feel that they are living in perpetual silence, not thinking about anything at all, their minds a blank. They feel bereft of ideas. They feel that what they need is an active mind.

But the fact is that they are suppressing their ideas behind a noisy mind whose noise they can no longer hear. They possess both of the things that they think they don't possess—ideas and a noisy mind—but they don't know it. One aspect of a chattering mind is that it can pose as silence.

A thousand monkeys are plaguing you, so you lock them away in a soundproof room next to you. Unfortunately, beyond that room is the place where your ideas reside. What have you accomplished? You have produced perfect silence and you are keeping your anxiety at bay, but you have no thoughts.

This is the essence of a too-quiet mind. Your mind was chattering so you walled off the chatter. In the process you walled yourself off from your own thoughts and feelings. Your thoughts are over there and between you and them are the monkeys, with whom you must deal.

Whether your mind is too noisy or too quiet, it amounts to the same problem: negative self-talk that needs addressing and exorcising.

90.

WRONG MIND: "I'm so upset by my unwillingness to do a careful job of marketing my writing that I want to strangle myself."

RIGHT MIND: "I am resolved to start fresh with marketing. The first thing I am going to do is take a careful inventory of my writing and ruthlessly retire those pieces that aren't strong. If nothing is left after that examination, I have some new writing to do."

91.

WRONG MIND: "My first book was no good. My second book was no good. Why should I write a third book?"

RIGHT MIND: "My apprenticeship continues and I am eager to write my third book."

92.

WRONG MIND: "I love to write long, descriptive passages, which I know editors will hate. So why should I bother writing?"

RIGHT MIND: "If my book is beautiful and strong, some editor will want it."

93.

WRONG MIND: "I don't deserve to call myself a writer."

RIGHT MIND: "I can call myself a writer or a mongoose, for all that matters. The only important thing is that I write."

94.

WRONG MIND: "There have been a thousand books written on my subject. What could I possibly add?"

RIGHT MIND: "My subject is evergreen and if I write a strong, smart, compelling book proposal my book will be wanted."

95.

WRONG MIND: "Nowadays you have to pledge that you will spend a billion dollars of your own money on promoting your book before editors will take an interest. That's absurd and offensive and I won't do it."

RIGHT MIND: "An editor needs to know that a book has real markets and that those real markets can be reached. If I can explain in a clear, compelling way who my readers will be and how they can be reached, I have a chance of getting editors interested in my book."

"Like totalitarian regimes,
the ego organizes knowledge
in a way that exalts itself,
distorts new information,
and revises past experiences
to justify its own premises."

DAVID FEINSTEIN

96.

WRONG MIND: "I've never won any writing awards, I've never had anything published, and no one knows my name. Why should an editor take an interest in my book?"

RIGHT MIND: "My first job is to write a book that starts out beautifully and that stays strong. My second job is to market it smartly and relentlessly to agents and editors. The rest I leave to the gods of whimsy."

97.

WRONG MIND: "I crave solitude but I also flee from solitude. I must be a nutcase."

RIGHT MIND: "As soon as I settle into solitude I get very anxious, fearing that I have nothing to say and that I'm about to make a mess. My job is to quiet my nerves, not to run out of the room."

98.

WRONG MIND: "I would never publish my book as an e-book. Nobody reads e-books and my chances of finding a real publisher would be ruined."

RIGHT MIND: "I am open to investigating every publishing possibility, including e-books. Maybe it's for me and maybe it isn't, but I won't dismiss it without looking into it."

99.

WRONG MIND: "I'm sick of the drivel I write."

RIGHT MIND: "I must be doing something to prevent myself from letting my best writing out. My hunch is that I'm not writing from the heart and not speaking my truth. Therefore my next piece will not be about some idea that interests me but will be the equivalent of a pool of my blood on the page."

100.

WRONG MIND: "I don't want to be a writer. I want to be normal."

RIGHT MIND: "It is much safer to wear the camouflage of the average person than to 'act special' and write. But in order to feel alive I need to make meaning by writing."

101.

WRONG MIND: "My contract says that my manuscript should be delivered by May 1, but I'm sure no one will mind if I get it in by late summer or by early fall at the latest."

RIGHT MIND: "It is very important that I deliver my manuscript on time. If I can't, I had better let my editor know."

102.

WRONG MIND: "My mother doesn't believe in me."

RIGHT MIND: "I am endeavoring to believe in myself."

103.

WRONG MIND: "My father doesn't believe in me."

RIGHT MIND: "I am endeavoring to believe in myself."

104.

WRONG MIND: "My mate doesn't believe in me."

RIGHT MIND: "I need a new mate."

Crying Shame

A writer wrote me:

For close to seven years now I've been blocked. My background is pretty much textbook. I'm a recovering addict—a survivor of at least sixteen years of sexual molestation. I was forbidden to write as a child and even had my writings ripped from notebooks and tacked to my bedroom wall (the entire wall was filled) when I was about fifteen. This was my punishment for my parents not liking my poetry and other things I had written at the time. Those pages were tacked to the wall for a month and shown to whomever happened to visit our house. Mustn't this have something to do with my fear of writing?

How can a person recover from being shamed in this way? How can such damage be undone? Maybe it would help to say, "I have been harmed and now the problem is my own personality. I have needles sticking me all over my body and when I even *think* about writing, the needles cause me excruciating pain. Can I remove the needles?"

Can this writer heal herself by right thinking, by choosing new thoughts? We can't say yes for sure, but we mustn't say no.

105.

WRONG MIND: "My publicist at Very Big Publishing asked if I could do a radio interview tomorrow morning at eight. Unfortunately, that's exactly the time I read the newspaper."

RIGHT MIND: "Although I get the jitters before interviews and therefore want to avoid them like the plague, I will seize every opportunity to help my book."

106.

WRONG MIND: "I am sending things out to editors half my age. No wonder they keep rejecting me."

RIGHT MIND: "Editors have no idea how old I am. They are just looking at the quality of the package. Besides, aren't Stephen King or Anne Rice older than many people in publishing?"

107.

WRONG MIND: "Once I get a few things published I'll be well on my way to a career in writing."

RIGHT MIND: "Every piece I write will probably have to

stand on its own merits until the end of time. I'm okay with that."

108.

WRONG MIND: "God, Dan just published another book! I'm going to die."

RIGHT MIND: "Even though I am disappointed and even humiliated by my lack of success, I will not give up."

109.

WRONG MIND: "I write for smart people. Therefore, my market is very small."

RIGHT MIND: "Maybe I mean that I'm the only smart person around? Is that the idiotic thing I'm saying?"

110.

WRONG MIND: "It's all right if the middle of my novel is a little boring. As a reader, I don't mind the boring parts."

"If I really mean that the middle of my novel is boring, I need to rewrite it. 'Boring' is neither a goal nor a plus."

111.

WRONG MIND: "I have no chance."
RIGHT MIND: "I still have hope."

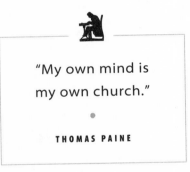

"My own mind is
my own church."

•

THOMAS PAINE

112.

WRONG MIND: "It's all right if readers find my main character uninteresting. After all, my prose is *so* beautiful."

RIGHT MIND: "Meaning first, beauty second. My novel will mean more to me—and to my readers—if the main character comes alive."

113.

WRONG MIND: "It's all right if there's no conflict in my novel, no arc, no character growth, no resolution. After all, my prose is *so* beautiful."

RIGHT MIND: "Meaning first, beauty second. My novel must mean as well as sing."

114.

WRONG MIND: "I just read about this eight-year-old girl who got a seventy-five-thousand-dollar advance for a book of her poetry. That makes me so crazy I may have to set my drapes on fire."

RIGHT MIND: "I look to the marketplace for information, not for sanity and certainly not for fairness."

115.

WRONG MIND: "I write serious things and the world only wants fluff."

RIGHT MIND: "I am not at war with fluff. That's not a war I could win! My only job is to do good work and find markets for that work, however large or small those markets may be."

116.

WRONG MIND: "I can't create a good plot."

RIGHT MIND: "Apparently spending five minutes trying to create a plot and then fleeing in confusion is not enough of an effort. I will stay put and learn to plot."

117.

WRONG MIND: "I'd love to write some self-help nonfiction, but I could never come up with all those exercises and vignettes."

RIGHT MIND: "Apparently spending five minutes trying to come up with exercises and vignettes and then fleeing in confusion is not enough of an effort. I will stay put and learn to write exercises and vignettes."

118.

WRONG MIND: "My historical romance is about thirty-five thousand words long. That's about sixty thousand words short, but I'm sure an editor will understand."

RIGHT MIND: "If I am writing in a genre, I will understand that genre and abide by its rules. If ninety-five thousand words are wanted, my novel will come in at ninety-five thousand words."

119.

WRONG MIND: "I'd like to write an article for my professional journal, but the subject matter bores me to death. I guess I'll skip it."

RIGHT MIND: "Sometimes I will write things that excite me and sometimes I will write things that bore me. All that matters is that I make a reasoned choice that takes my career needs into account."

120.

WRONG MIND: "Once I appear on *The Oprah Winfrey Show* I will have it made. Therefore, I'm going to build a shrine to Oprah in my living room and begin worshiping."

RIGHT MIND: "Better to write than to fantasize."

121.

WRONG MIND: "I've decided to write a postmodern mystery in which it is impossible to tell who died, who committed the crime, or *if* there was a crime. I'm sure an editor will understand my intentions and love that I'm deconstructing the genre."

RIGHT MIND: "I can write a postmodern mystery if I like, but I can't act like I'm doing editors a favor. Since most editors will reject it out of hand, I'll have to think twice about whether I'm doing *myself* any great favor."

Just Listening

Say "I would like to work on my novel" or "I would like to start a short story" or whatever is appropriate. Then just listen for your response.

If you hear yourself say "All right!" or "Yes!" that is right mind. If you hear anything else, you are giving yourself the wrong message.

But what is that message exactly? Try to listen. There may be feelings but no words, which means that you must listen to your body. There may be very simple words like "no" or "can't." There may be soliloquies as long and complicated as anything in *Finnegans Wake*.

It is vital that you hear what you are saying to yourself about the idea of writing and about your capabilities as a writer. This is not self-obsessive, self-referential, or narcissistic. This is common sense. How can you distinguish right thinking from wrong thinking if you do not know what you are thinking?

122.

WRONG MIND: "If I sold my book, I'd have to do interviews—and I'm no public speaker. Therefore, I won't write it."

RIGHT MIND: "I will write my book and I will pray that I get a chance to speak about it."

123.

WRONG MIND: "The publishing world is treating me unfairly."

RIGHT MIND: "The publishing world is entirely indifferent to my existence. So is the universe, for that matter. None of that will stop me from writing or marketing my writing."

124.

WRONG MIND: "My personality is the pits. I'm my own worst enemy and I will never realize my dreams."

RIGHT MIND: "I must believe in the possibility of personal change and I must begin to change."

125.

WRONG MIND: "Whenever I try to write, my mind wanders. I have no control over where it will go or when it will come back."

RIGHT MIND: "I can focus and I can concentrate."

126.

WRONG MIND: "Since nobody has ever encouraged me, I don't have the internal resources to write."

RIGHT MIND: "I am my own best friend and advocate."

127.

WRONG MIND: "My editor left the publishing company and now my book is orphaned. Therefore, I am doomed and I might as well not finish revising it."

RIGHT MIND: "I will finish my book on time, try to find a new champion for it within the publishing house, and hire an outside editor if that becomes necessary. I am not giving up on this book."

128.

WRONG MIND: "The standard publishing contract is an insult and an indignity and I will either get every word I don't like changed or not bother to publish."

RIGHT MIND: "I will keep my eye on the advance, the delivery date, the option clause, and about three or four other crucial things, and not worry too much about the rest of the contract."

129.

WRONG MIND: "My head hurts. I can't write today."

RIGHT MIND: "I'm going to take two aspirin and pick up my pen as soon as the pain stops."

130.

WRONG MIND: "I can't decide whether John should be a transvestite or a transsexual. The choice is so confusing that I think I will put the novel aside for six months and come back to it in September."

RIGHT MIND: "I can't decide whether John should be a transvestite or a transsexual. The choice is so confusing that I think I will put the novel aside for the evening and come back to it in the morning."

131.

WRONG MIND: "My good friend Sally hated my latest story. Therefore, she is now my worst enemy."

RIGHT MIND: "Friendships don't hang in the balance when I show people my work."

132.

WRONG MIND: "If I could figure out how to arrange my poems, I would have my collection ready."

RIGHT MIND: "I will figure out how to arrange my poems and I will get my collection ready."

133.

WRONG MIND: "I think I'll send along a box of chocolates with every query letter I send out."

RIGHT MIND: "When my books sells, I will definitely send my agent and my editor chocolates."

Psychological Problems?

Are there psychological problems behind your mind chatter and wrong thinking? Or are they merely due to everyday human nature? After all, it is human nature to avoid uncharted waters. It is human nature not to think long and hard. It is human nature to keep the ego protected. Before you blame your wrong thinking on psychological trauma and damage, consider the possibility that you are being quite stubbornly human.

Simple human nature will keep more people from writing than will psychological problems.

134.

WRONG MIND: "I must stop now."

RIGHT MIND: "Do I really need to stop now?"

135.

WRONG MIND: "I must stop now."

RIGHT MIND: "Can't I do a little more?"

136.

WRONG MIND: "I must stop now."

RIGHT MIND: "I need to stretch for a second."

137.

WRONG MIND: "I must stop now."

RIGHT MIND: "I mustn't stop now."

"Nobody is ever met at the airport
when beginning a new adventure."

•

ELIZABETH FERNEA

138.

WRONG MIND: "I have a great idea for a screenplay. With all that option money just around the corner, I think I'll go out and charge a few things to my credit card."

RIGHT MIND: "I am going to turn my great idea for a screenplay into a great screenplay."

139.

WRONG MIND: "I've been getting a lot of needed research done. Three more years of research and I'll be ready to start making sense of this book."

RIGHT MIND: "I'm ready to start making at least some tentative sense of all the information I've been gathering."

140.

WRONG MIND: "I can't possibly write after the sun goes down."

RIGHT MIND: "I will train myself to write morning, noon, or night."

141.

WRONG MIND: "I can't possibly write before breakfast."

RIGHT MIND: "I will train myself to write morning, noon, or night."

142.

WRONG MIND: "If I don't write, I can't fail."

RIGHT MIND: "If I don't write, I can't experience the profound joy of writing well."

143.

WRONG MIND: "When, as an experiment, a writer retypes a novel that was well-known forty years ago and submits it to editors, they never recognize it and they never like it enough to publish it. Editors are frauds and idiots."

RIGHT MIND: "Why should I expect a thirty-year-old editor who majored in art history to know classic novels from forty years ago? I could read my *own* novel and not recognize it! I can't waste my energy proving to myself that editors are too foolish to see my genius."

144.

WRONG MIND: "I'm too angry to write."

RIGHT MIND: "I *am* angry, but I can use my anger to motivate myself and to power my writing."

145.

WRONG MIND: "I'm missing a word of my poem. I can't write until it arrives."

RIGHT MIND: "I'm missing a word of my poem. While I'm waiting for it to arrive, I can work on something else."

146.

WRONG MIND: "I keep writing the same thing. I appear to have only one note to sing."

RIGHT MIND: "I will continue to mine this vein as long as it holds meaning for me."

147.

WRONG MIND: "Dan just published *another* book. I'm going to Amazon *right now* and give it a terrible review."

RIGHT MIND: "Let me get back to my novel."

148.

WRONG MIND: "I can't write because I don't know."

RIGHT MIND: "I can write even though I don't know."

149.

WRONG MIND: "I can't write because I don't know."

RIGHT MIND: "I can write exactly because I don't know. If I knew already, how bored I'd be!"

150.

WRONG MIND: "I can't write because I don't know."
RIGHT MIND: "I will only know once I write."

Don't Know

If you are afraid of "don't know," change your attitude.

There are so many things that we don't know that if we fear all that, we live in perpetual fear. We don't know what tomorrow will bring. We don't know whether we will succeed or fail. We don't know if our children will have good luck. We don't know if what we are writing will turn out fine.

Once you accept that there are a million things you don't know, your anxiety shrinks. Accept and surrender. You just do not know. You have decisions to make, courage to show, and a heart and a brain to use. Beyond that, you don't know and you can't know.

If you are waiting to know, you have created your own obstacle to knowing.

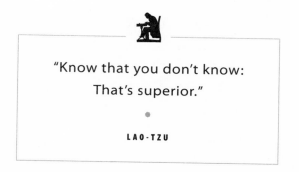

"Know that you don't know:
That's superior."

•

LAO-TZU

151.

WRONG MIND: "I know that my book doesn't start out with a bang, but I'm sure editors will have the patience to get to the good parts."

RIGHT MIND: "The first pages of my book are going to be so strong that you could build a skyscraper on them."

152.

WRONG MIND: "I think I'll start out my query letter by apologizing for not having had anything published yet."

RIGHT MIND: "The job of the query letter is to sell me and my project, period."

153.

WRONG MIND: "I think I'll start out my query letter by demanding to be treated fairly."

RIGHT MIND: "The job of the query letter is to sell me and my project, period."

154.

WRONG MIND: "I can't write today."

BETTER MIND: "I can write a little today."

EVEN BETTER MIND: "I can write a lot today."

155.

WRONG MIND: "I always make messes."

BETTER MIND: "I sometimes make messes."

EVEN BETTER MIND: "What are messes?"

156.

WRONG MIND: "I'm no thinker."

BETTER MIND: "I can think."

EVEN BETTER MIND: "I love to think."

157.

WRONG MIND: "My agent says that she is disappointed in my latest manuscript and can't represent it. I should call her and insult her."

RIGHT MIND: "I may need a new agent, I may need a second agent to handle this project, I may need to try to sell this myself, I may need to revise it and improve it, or I may need to abandon it. Those are my options."

158.

WRONG MIND: "The comments my editor made on my manuscript were very cruel. She may be right in her opinions, but she has no right to be so rude."

RIGHT MIND: "I am so much more evolved than my editor that I can take her rudeness with a grain of salt."

159.

WRONG MIND: "If I became a Buddhist monk, I would acquire the discipline I need to write."

RIGHT MIND: "Writing discipline is writing discipline. To achieve it, I write."

160.

WRONG MIND: "If I achieved a black belt in karate, I would acquire the discipline I need to write."

RIGHT MIND: "Writing discipline is writing discipline. To achieve it, I write."

161.

WRONG MIND: "If I became a champion marathon runner, I would acquire the discipline I need to write."

RIGHT MIND: "Writing discipline is writing discipline. To achieve it, I write."

162.

WRONG MIND: "I refuse to explain why I am writing a nonfiction book about 1952. It should be obvious."

RIGHT MIND: "I will reveal my reasons for writing what I am writing. This helps others and may also help me understand whether or not what I am attempting is a good idea."

163.

WRONG MIND: "I refuse to explain why I am writing a play about lesbian politics. It should be obvious."

RIGHT MIND: "I will reveal my reasons for writing what I am writing. This helps others and may also help me understand whether or not what I am attempting is a good idea."

164.

WRONG MIND: "I grew up in a dull place doing dull things and thinking dull thoughts. Therefore, my dream of writing is ridiculous."

RIGHT MIND: "I am not really dull and I know it! I must stop characterizing my childhood and my upbringing as fatal impediments to writing."

What Affirming Means

Affirming is not the same thing as speaking to yourself in a kind and friendly way. When you affirm something, you solemnly declare that you are equal to a challenge or that you intend to grow equal to that challenge. You assert that you are on a certain track or that you will get on that track. You announce that you mean to better yourself and move in a new direction. Your affirmations support you but they do not let you off the hook.

After giving a workshop, I received the following letter.

I wanted to share with you some of the affirmations I've written since Saturday:
- *I write magic!*
- *I am open to serendipity.*
- *I will hold the dream.*

- *I do not fear success.*
- *The choice is mine to make.*
- *I am committed to mastering the craft of writing.*
- *I will live my life.*
- *I pledge allegiance to the truth.*
- *I will write outside the lines.*

You untie a hundred knots when you create simple sentences that herald and support your goals.

165.

WRONG MIND: "After I grade my students' papers I have no brain cells left with which to write."

RIGHT MIND: "I will write first thing in the morning, at four A.M. if necessary."

166.

WRONG MIND: "I need to nag my children about their dirty rooms."

RIGHT MIND: "I need to write."

167.

WRONG MIND: "I need to nag my husband about the state of the lawn."

RIGHT MIND: "I need to write."

168.

WRONG MIND: "I need to nag my wife for sex."

RIGHT MIND: "I need to write."

169.

WRONG MIND: "I need to nag myself about all the chores that aren't getting done."

RIGHT MIND: "I need to write."

"'Know thyself'?
If I knew myself,
I'd run away."

GOETHE

170.

WRONG MIND: "I can't describe things."

RIGHT MIND: "I should practice describing things."

171.

WRONG MIND: "I can't create rounded characters."

RIGHT MIND: "I should practice creating rounded characters."

172.

WRONG MIND: "I can't foreshadow."

RIGHT MIND: "I should practice foreshadowing."

173.

WRONG MIND: "I'm looking forward to that weeklong conference so very much! Nothing but other writers, no chores, and the chance to write!"

RIGHT MIND: "I'm looking forward to that week-long conference so very much! But I have to be careful and I have to be mindful. There will be all those other writers to spar with, drink with, and flirt with. There will be all that silence. There will be many opportunities to nap and to take long walks. I hope I'm up to the challenge of writing in such circumstances and I may want to plan my writing schedule *now*."

174.

WRONG MIND: "I need to take a break. I've been writing for almost two hours!"

RIGHT MIND: "I need to take a *short* break. I've been writing for almost two hours!"

175.

WRONG MIND: "I was taught not to stand out in a crowd. I learned that lesson very well—all too well."

RIGHT MIND: "I am teaching myself a new lesson—that I intend to stand out from the crowd."

176.

WRONG MIND: "I was taught to not make waves. I learned that lesson very well—all too well."

RIGHT MIND: "I am teaching myself a new lesson—that I will make any waves that need making."

177.

WRONG MIND: "I was taught to keep secrets. I learned that lesson very well—all too well."

RIGHT MIND: "I am teaching myself a new lesson—that some secrets must be revealed."

178.

WRONG MIND: "John says I should change the point of view of my novel. I suppose I should."

RIGHT MIND: "What John says rings no bell with me, so I will just file his comment away."

179.

WRONG MIND: "Harriet says I should add more drama to my memoir. She feels that right now it's boring. I suppose I should."

RIGHT MIND: "What Harriet says rings a bell and is exactly what I was thinking. I *will* add more drama!"

180.

WRONG MIND: "My writing teacher says that I should stop writing. He claims that I have no talent."

RIGHT MIND: "He can fry in hell."

A Right Thinker's Pledge

"I will answer every charge I make against myself the instant I make it. If I hear myself saying, 'You are too stupid to write this book,' I will instantly respond, 'No, I am not too stupid.' If I hear myself saying, 'You are too lazy to do good work,' I will instantly respond, 'No, I am not too lazy.' If I hear myself saying, 'I don't feel up to thinking,' I will exclaim, 'I am off to think!' I will refute every wrong thought the instant I hear it."

181.

WRONG MIND: "I love to write in cafés but when I go to a café I just daydream, eavesdrop on conversations, or try to look cool. I should never go to cafés to write."

RIGHT MIND: "Going out to write is a blessed thing, but my new deal with myself is that when I go out I *will* write, at least for the first hour."

182.

WRONG MIND: "I love to write at the beach, but when I go to the beach I mostly soak up the sun and nap. I should never go to the beach to write."

RIGHT MIND: "Going out to write is a blessed thing, but my new deal with myself is that when I go out I *will* write, at least for the first hour."

183.

WRONG MIND: "This sentence is killing me! I have to go to the emergency room!"

RIGHT MIND: "Hush, and stop dramatizing!"

184.

WRONG MIND: "This paragraph is killing me! I need first aid and a bottle of whiskey."

RIGHT MIND: "Hush, and stop dramatizing!"

185.

WRONG MIND: "This chapter is killing me! I will never get it right and when I go to my grave it will still be in its present crappy state!"

RIGHT MIND: "Hush, and stop dramatizing!"

"Teach yourself to work
in uncertainty."

BERNARD MALAMUD

186.

WRONG MIND: "I want to write a book about what helps ex-cons stay out of prison, but I don't know enough. Therefore, I can't write that book."

RIGHT MIND: "Maybe I don't know enough, but I do have some hunches and some hypotheses. I can at least get what I do know down on paper and see what I've got."

187.

WRONG MIND: "I want to write a book about what helps ex-cons stay out of prison, but I don't know enough. Therefore, I can't write that book."

RIGHT MIND: "Maybe I don't know enough now, but I am going to do some intensive and rapid research and quickly get a handle on what is currently known."

188.

WRONG MIND: "I want to write a book about what helps ex-cons stay out of prison, but I don't know enough. Therefore, I can't write that book."

RIGHT MIND: "Of course I don't know enough yet. There-fore, I think I'll interview several ex-cons who have stayed out of prison for ten years or more and see what they have to say about what helped them not commit a new crime."

189.

WRONG MIND: "I want to write a book about what helps ex-cons stay out of prison, but I don't know enough. Therefore, I can't write that book."

RIGHT MIND: "Maybe I don't know enough and maybe I do. However, I'm certain that my fears and doubts are what are really stopping me, not my lack of knowledge. I need courage and I need to begin some-where."

190.

WRONG MIND: "My book will be experimental."

RIGHT MIND: "My book will be experimental and, more important, good."

191.

WRONG MIND: "My book will be iconoclastic."

RIGHT MIND: "My book will be iconoclastic and, more important, good."

192.

WRONG MIND: "My book will be avant-garde."

RIGHT MIND: "My book will be avant-garde and, more important, good."

193.

WRONG MIND: "My book about New England inns must come with color photos."

RIGHT MIND: "I would love it if my book comes with color photos but, unless I'm self-publishing, I'm not in control of that."

194.

WRONG MIND: "My book of poetry must be set in fourteen-point Century Schoolbook font."

RIGHT MIND: "I would love it if my book were set in the type of my choice but, unless I'm self-publishing, I'm not in control of that."

195.

WRONG MIND: "My novel must have a yellow-and-indigo cover."

RIGHT MIND: "I would love the cover of my book to be exactly what I want but, unless I'm self-publishing, I'm not in control of that."

Disputing Thoughts

It seems quite strange to dispute our own thoughts, like something you would see in a Monty Python sketch: a person wrestling himself to the ground or a person giving himself a good tongue-lashing. We grow up supposing that our thoughts are accurate—that is a cat, that is a lot of homework, that is a funny television show. It rarely occurs to us to wonder, "Is that a lot of homework or do I just fear math?" or, "Is that a funny television show or am I just being seduced by the laugh track?" We go along uncritically buying our own thoughts, like a shopper who will put anything into his cart.

Then one day we notice a wrong thought. We say that we are angry but we know that we are sad. We say that the book we are reading is a classic but we know that we are bored. We say that we have ruined everything but we know that we have only made a small mistake. Over time, we begin to see that our thoughts may be right or our thoughts may be wrong. This is a giant insight!

Next we learn that we can dispute these wrong thoughts. We can say, "No, I am sad." We can say, "I don't need to finish reading this book." We can say, "Really, the mistake was nothing!" We can say the right thing and do ourselves infinitely less harm.

196.

WRONG MIND: "The first thing I do each morning is write in my journal. The second thing I do is my yoga practice. The third thing I do is get ready for my day job."

RIGHT MIND: "The first thing I do each morning is write on my current project."

197.

WRONG MIND: "Editors know everything. The fact that they take no interest in my work proves that I'm no good."

RIGHT MIND: "Editors know many things but certainly not everything. I will not let editorial silence or a particular editor's opinion erode my self-confidence."

198.

WRONG MIND: "Editors know nothing. The fact that they take no interest in my work only confirms my low opinion of them."

RIGHT MIND: "Editors do not know everything but they certainly know some things. The fact that they take no interest in my work is important information and I need to figure out what it means."

199.

WRONG MIND: "I don't know when to use 'that' and when to use 'which.' I am no writer."

RIGHT MIND: "I have something to say and I will say it well."

200.

WRONG MIND: "I don't know where the commas go. I am no writer."

RIGHT MIND: "I have something to say and I will say it well."

201.

WRONG MIND: "I don't know when to use 'you and I' and when to use 'you and me.' I am no writer."

RIGHT MIND: "I have something to say and I will say it well."

202.

WRONG MIND: "I want to write a screenplay about a band of boys in Sweden in 1942 who managed to save thousands of Swedish art treasures from the Nazis. But for every ten thousand screenplays that get written, maybe one movie gets made. So what's the point of trying?"

RIGHT MIND: "I have the plot and the characters for my screenplay in mind and if I stay focused I could do ten pages a weekend for twelve weekends running and have a draft of my screenplay done in three months. Can't I 'squander' twelve weekends on this dream, and then do one terrific job of marketing it?"

203.

WRONG MIND: "I only want to drink and sleep around. That's why I'm choosing the writing life. It's not that I want to write."

RIGHT MIND: "The truth is, I really want to write."

204.

WRONG MIND: "I only want to avoid working for some corporation or doing some other idiotic, time-serving thing with my life. It's not that I want to write."

RIGHT MIND: "The truth is, I really want to write."

205.

WRONG MIND: "I only want to feel free and special. It's not that I want to write."

RIGHT MIND: "The truth is, I really want to write."

206.

WRONG MIND: "I'm looking forward to the writing retreat in Maui next year that I enrolled in. I'm sure that will get me back on track with my book."

RIGHT MIND: "I'm looking forward to the writing retreat I'm planning for myself next weekend, here on my porch or at the caféteria of my local college. I'm sure that will get me back on track with my book."

207.

WRONG MIND: "One editor says that she hates it when an author claims that his book is 'the first one ever to do such-and-such' or 'the only one of its kind.' Another editor says we should make sure to express how our book is unique. Are they trying to drive me nuts?"

RIGHT MIND: "They mean, 'Be compelling and say it well.' That's the long and the short of it."

208.

WRONG MIND: "I have no future in writing."

RIGHT MIND: "I just may have an excellent future in writing. I will have to wait and see."

209.

WRONG MIND: "I have no future in writing."

RIGHT MIND: "I have a passionate present in writing."

210.

WRONG MIND: "If I write very diffidently, no one can charge me with posing as an expert."

RIGHT MIND: "If I write too diffidently, no agent or editor will take me seriously."

Substituting Better Thoughts

One day you do a nice job of disputing a wrong thought. You see right through to the issue underneath and exclaim to the thought, "Gotcha!" But your wrong thought gets the last laugh: "Okay, buddy, if you aren't going to entertain me as your thought, what *will* you think?"

The first time or two, you aren't sure. What is the better thought? Then you get the hang of it. The better thought is the one that doesn't knock you down a peg. The better thought is the one that promotes your writing and your writing career. The better thought is the one that helps you concentrate, that prevents you from running away, that brings you back after a pratfall.

A new day dawns and you realize that you haven't been crafting thought substitutes for a while, because you've had no occasion to need them. You've just been thinking right.

211.

WRONG MIND: "I would never go to a writers' conference. Only old people and losers go to writers' conferences."

RIGHT MIND: "I know plenty and I have plenty to learn."

212.

WRONG MIND: "I would never take a writing workshop, not even from a Nobel Prize winner. Workshops are for weaklings."

RIGHT MIND: "I know plenty and I have plenty to learn."

213.

WRONG MIND: "I would never listen to an editor. If editors could write, they would be writers."

RIGHT MIND: "I know plenty and I have plenty to learn."

214.

WRONG MIND: "I'm under too much pressure at work and the stress is just as high when I get home. I can't possibly write."

RIGHT MIND: "Maybe I can write for five or ten minutes a day. That would be a start—and a genuine accomplishment."

215.

WRONG MIND: "If I don't write this week, that's proof that I'm a fraud and a liar."

RIGHT MIND: "I will write this week. Whether I do or I don't, I will write next week—without calling myself any bad names in between."

216.

WRONG MIND: "I have too many writing projects on my plate. I can't seem to choose which one to work on first."

RIGHT MIND: "I can choose."

217.

WRONG MIND: "I'm a psychotherapist, not a writer."

RIGHT MIND: "I can have two careers. In fact, I would love to have two careers."

218.

WRONG MIND: "I'm an elementary school teacher, not a writer."

RIGHT MIND: "I can have two careers. In fact, I would love to have two careers."

219.

WRONG MIND: "I haven't written for a week. That must mean that I will never write again."

RIGHT MIND: "I am very ready to write after a week of not writing."

220.

WRONG MIND: "I haven't written for six months. That must mean that I will never write again."

RIGHT MIND: "I am *very* ready to write after six months of not writing."

"Clarity is
a way of life."

•

KEORAPETSE KGOSITSILE

221.

WRONG MIND: "I have written a beautiful poem, but it will never be published."

RIGHT MIND: "I have written a beautiful poem and perhaps it will be published."

222.

WRONG MIND: "I have written an excellent short story, but it will never be published."

RIGHT MIND: "I have written an excellent short story and perhaps it will be published."

223.

WRONG MIND: "I have written a darn good first novel, but it will never be published."

RIGHT MIND: "I have written a darn good first novel and perhaps it will be published."

224.

WRONG MIND: "My mate belittles me. That breaks my heart and shrivels me up. I am left unable to write."

RIGHT MIND: "It is not all right that my mate belittles me. I must make that stop, one way or the other, and I must write."

225.

WRONG MIND: "I am too fat to write."

RIGHT MIND: "Let's see. Balzac. Orson Welles. Marlon Brando. Alfred Hitchcock. You can't be heavy and be creative? What I really mean is, 'I am so down on myself.' Well, I want to write and I will write!"

226.

WRONG MIND: "My father beat all the writing out of me."
RIGHT MIND: "I am healing and I am writing."

Hard Truths

I once met with a blocked artist who had painted when he was in his 20s. When he was in his 30s, he'd made pencil drawings. He came to see me when he was 40, not having produced any art for a year.

He showed me slides of his artwork. The paintings and drawings were "mythological" and made reference to occult systems, fairy tales, and so on.

One painting was different. I asked him about it.

"That one? The others I would do in a few days or a week, based on ideas I had. That one took me almost two years. I was breaking up with my girlfriend that whole time and I kept adding and adding to that painting. It was like a record of the breakup."

"You need to stop with the mythology," I told him, "and tell the truth, like you do in that painting."

Possibly he hated me for saying that. Then again, maybe he didn't. What he said was, "I know." At the end of the session he said, "I have a lot to think about." Then he gave me a hug.

Avoiding and denying the truth always lead to wrong thinking. Revealing the truth to yourself leads to right thinking.

227.

WRONG MIND: "I want to write about my mother, but I have to wait until she dies so I won't hurt her feelings."

RIGHT MIND: "I have important things to write about right now and I will find a way to write about them."

228.

WRONG MIND: "It would be nice to gather some statistics on the number of insomniacs in the United States to include in my *Great Sleep* book proposal, but I can't be bothered."

RIGHT MIND: "I can be bothered."

229.

WRONG MIND: "It would be great to get an early endorsement for my *Great Sleep* book, but I don't know the right people."

RIGHT MIND: "I will figure out which experts to approach and I will approach them."

230.

WRONG MIND: "It might be smart to write a second chapter of my *Great Sleep* book, since the one I'm including with the proposal is so short. But I don't feel up to it."

RIGHT MIND: "I am up to it."

231.

WRONG MIND: "My mind is on auto-scan, always darting around. I have no attention span."

RIGHT MIND: "Anxiety, anxiety, anxiety. I just need to quiet my nerves and stay put."

232.

WRONG MIND: "I must have attention deficit disorder. I can't concentrate on anything for even two seconds."

RIGHT MIND: "When something interests me, I concentrate beautifully. The culprit is anxiety. I just need to quiet my nerves and stay put."

233.

WRONG MIND: "I hate solitude."

RIGHT MIND: "Anxiety again! I hate the anxiety that wells up when I try to be quiet and write. But I can manage my anxiety."

234.

WRONG MIND: "The fact that I am well-off financially prevents me from writing. I should give away my money and become a wandering monk."

RIGHT MIND: "The problem is not too much money or anything of that sort. The problem is fear. I need courage and I need to write."

235.

WRONG MIND: "I should be an expatriate and live in Paris. But I don't like the French."

RIGHT MIND: "There may be good reasons to make a big geographic move, but there are no good reasons not to write right now."

236.

WRONG MIND: "It is humiliating that I want so badly to write but never do."

RIGHT MIND: "Humiliated or not, I will write today."

237.

WRONG MIND: "My play requires seventeen sets and ninety-two actors. No problem there."

RIGHT MIND: "Of course that's a problem. Stubbornness is fine. Artistic integrity is fine. Thinking big is fine. But I need to be clear that I am writing a play that no artistic director can afford to stage. So what are my intentions? Do I want to thumb my nose at the marketplace? Play at heroism? I would like to know what I'm thinking and what I'm intending."

238.

WRONG MIND: "In my field, it's publish or perish, but I have nothing to say. Therefore, I must perish."

RIGHT MIND: "If nothing in my field interests me enough to write about, I have a bigger problem than not writing. I am either in the wrong field or much more frightened than I imagined."

239.

WRONG MIND: "I belong in the back of the pack, not in the front."

RIGHT MIND: "I belong up front."

240.

WRONG MIND: "I belong in a closet, not out in the light of day."

RIGHT MIND: "No closets for me!"

241.

WRONG MIND: "I belong at the bottom, not at the top."
RIGHT MIND: "I am rising with the cream."

How Unreasonable

Aaron Beck is a well-known exponent of cognitive therapy. In his book *Depression: Causes and Treatment*, he wrote the following about a series of sessions with a patient:

A patient reported that he felt blue every time he made a mistake. He could not understand why he should feel this way. He fully accepted the notion that there was nothing wrong with making mistakes and that it was an inevitable part of living. He was instructed to focus on his thoughts the next time he felt an unpleasant affect in connection with making a mistake.

At the next interview he reported the observation that whenever he made a mistake he would think, "I'm a dope" or, "I never do anything right" or, "How can anybody be so dumb?" After having one of these thoughts he would become depressed. By becoming aware of the self-criticisms, however, he was able to recognize how unreasonable they were.

This recognition seemed to remove the sting from his blue reactions.

When a self-abusive thought appears, shake your head and say, "How unreasonable."

242.

WRONG MIND: "I am not ready to write this book. I need another twenty years of living first. Therefore, I won't write."

RIGHT MIND: "I am ready to write the book that I am able to write at this stage of my development."

243.

WRONG MIND: "The nineteenth-century novel is dead. I want to write nineteenth-century novels. That makes me a dinosaur and, worse, a fool."

RIGHT MIND: "I can write excellent twenty-first century novels full of atmosphere, ideas, plot, characters, and anything else I require."

244.

WRONG MIND: "I have twenty-six years of journals, ninety volumes in all. Maybe I can publish them."

RIGHT MIND: "Somewhere in these journals may be the starting point for an excellent book."

245.

WRONG MIND: "I can start things, but I never finish them. I have no stamina, no discipline, and no courage."

RIGHT MIND: "There is no doubt that I am troubled by my own personality, but from this day forward I will begin to complete things."

246.

WRONG MIND: "I have twelve thousand four hundred thirty-three writing fragments accumulated. Maybe I can market them as a collection."

RIGHT MIND: "Somewhere in these fragments may be the starting point for an excellent book."

247.

WRONG MIND: "I want to write a book about trained crickets, but who would buy a whole book about trained crickets?"

RIGHT MIND: "An excellent book about trained crickets might sell. I can afford to take two months and put together a book proposal."

248.

WRONG MIND: "I want to write a novel about time passing slowly, but who would buy a novel about time passing slowly?

RIGHT, MIND: "If it is really in my heart to write this novel, then I will write it."

249.

WRONG MIND: "I want to write an article about broccoli, but who cares about broccoli?"

RIGHT MIND: "I can write and sell an article about broccoli."

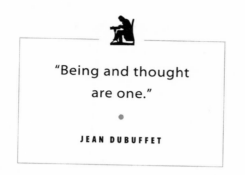

> "Being and thought
> are one."
>
> •
>
> **JEAN DUBUFFET**

250.

WRONG MIND: "The desire to write is a manifestation of ego and ego is a trap."

RIGHT MIND: "Desire is both human and fine. I have nothing against orgasms or bestsellers."

251.

WRONG MIND: "Writing depresses me. Therefore, I shouldn't write."

RIGHT MIND: "Depression is a real problem for me, but am I really sure that writing is the source of my depression? Or might it be part of the cure?"

252.

WRONG MIND: "It takes courage to write and I'm a coward. That explains why I don't write."

RIGHT MIND: "It took courage even to say that! I must have a reservoir of untapped courage."

253.

WRONG MIND: "My college major was business administration. Why should I expect that I can write well?"

RIGHT MIND: "Writing is about thinking. Am I saying that I can't think?"

254.

WRONG MIND: "I'm a nurse. Why should I expect that I can write well?"

RIGHT MIND: "Writing is about thinking. Am I saying that I can't think?"

255.

WRONG MIND: "I'm such a beginner! I've written virtually nothing so far."

RIGHT MIND: "I can start to write at any time if I am willing to think."

Activities

The following are some activities that I have done in creativity coaching sessions that have had a great impact on my clients.

I have clapped while a client tried to write, so as to investigate distraction. I have stood with a client at the edge of a rug, as if we were at the edge of a cliff, to vicariously experience the vertigo of leaping into a creative project. I have suggested to a writer feeling unsure about what path to take with her children's book, "Okay, you be the badger and I'll be the raccoon. What should we talk about?" I have offered an actor who wanted to direct, but who didn't feel powerful enough to direct, permission to direct me. "Okay, direct me around the room. Send me from one place to another, tell me what you want me to do, tell me what you want me to say."

Consider what activities will help you acquire right mind. Then do them.

256.

WRONG MIND: "My sister is an excellent writer. No family should have more than one writer in it. Therefore, I won't write."

RIGHT MIND: "I am permitted to write."

257.

WRONG MIND: "My father is an excellent writer. Since I can't compete with him, I shouldn't write."

RIGHT MIND: "I am permitted to write."

258.

WRONG MIND: "Mary in my writing group suggested that I cut John out of my novel. Her comment hurt!"

RIGHT MIND: "What hurts is that Mary is right. That means that I have tons of new work to do on my novel, but I will do it."

259.

WRONG MIND: "That agent said that my novel started too slowly. I should shred the whole manuscript."

RIGHT MIND: "That agent said that my novel started too slowly. I need to consider if she may be right and, if she is, what I can do to improve it."

260.

WRONG MIND: "Agents and editors only want bestsellers. My book won't appeal to them."

RIGHT MIND: "Agents and editors want good books with real markets. I will make my book good and clearly describe its markets."

261.

WRONG MIND: "I don't know how to fix my book. I'm paralyzed."

RIGHT MIND: "These troubles are part of the process. I have no answers this split second, but I will not abandon this book prematurely or call myself dirty names."

262.

WRONG MIND: "The piece I am writing is too difficult. It is beyond me."

RIGHT MIND: "It is not beyond me."

263.

WRONG MIND: "I removed the parts of my novel that I didn't like and it turns out that there is virtually nothing left. I'm devastated!"

RIGHT MIND: "That was brave of me, though the results are painful to behold. After I lick my wounds I will bravely begin a second draft."

264.

WRONG MIND: "Rejection hurts too much."

BETTER MIND: "I can survive rejection."

EVEN BETTER MIND: "Rejection is not a word in my vocabulary."

265.

WRONG MIND: "On Sunday I have to do laundry and clean the house."

BETTER MIND: "On Sunday I am going to write, do laundry, and clean the house."

EVEN BETTER MIND: "On Sunday I am going to write a lot, do laundry, and clean the house."

266.

WRONG MIND: "I can't write. I only have an hour."

BETTER MIND: "I have an hour. I can write."

EVEN BETTER MIND: "An hour! How splendid! So much writing time!"

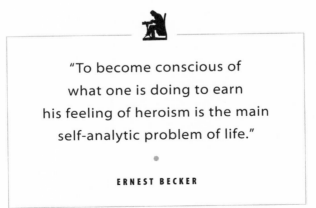

"To become conscious of
what one is doing to earn
his feeling of heroism is the main
self-analytic problem of life."

ERNEST BECKER

267.

WRONG MIND: "Every agent has told me that first novels are too hard to sell. What do they know?"

RIGHT MIND: "I believe in my novel and I will work incredibly hard to sell it."

268.

WRONG MIND: "Every agent has told me that first novels are too hard to sell. Therefore, I will burn my manuscript."

RIGHT MIND: "I believe in my novel and I will work incredibly hard to sell it."

269.

WRONG MIND: "Every agent has told me that first novels are too hard to sell. Therefore, I will put it in a drawer and begin a second novel."

RIGHT MIND: "I will work hard to sell my first novel and I will begin my second novel."

Unlimited Time

One day I received the following letter:

I am a fifty-year-old woman who did well early in life in the field of literature—graduate school, fellowships, teaching composition on the university level, the whole bit—and who gave it up to marry and raise a family. Now I'm finding it difficult, with unlimited time, no money problems, no need for "day jobs," and also no family any more to look after, to make the transition to creative writing, the one thing I wanted to do all along! I cannot seem to get myself to sit at the computer and complete a story of my own.

Wouldn't it be useful to know the contents of this would-be writer's mind? What wrong things would we hear? Unlimited time is nothing, only another pain, if your mind is your enemy. However, if you are thinking right, unlimited time is such a blessing!

270.

WRONG MIND: "I am a freak. I belong in a sideshow, not in front of a computer!"

RIGHT MIND: "I am a human being and I have things to say."

271.

WRONG MIND: "I am too young to write."
RIGHT MIND: "I am ready to write."

272.

WRONG MIND: "I am too old to write."
RIGHT MIND: "I am ready to write."

273.

WRONG MIND: "I need to find a job and make some money. Enough with trying to write!"
RIGHT MIND: "I will find a job and I will also write, if only for fifteen or twenty minutes a day or for a few hours on the weekend."

274.

WRONG MIND: "Writing used to be so much easier. Now it's painfully hard. Maybe I was never meant to write."

RIGHT MIND: "Maybe it's my self-talk that's gotten progressively more negative over the years. I had better see if *that's* the problem."

275.

WRONG MIND: "I've failed too many times. I've had it."

RIGHT MIND: "Yes, I'm sad and disappointed. But I'm excising 'failed' from my vocabulary!"

276.

WRONG MIND: "Writing is a serious undertaking and it's absurd to take life that seriously."

RIGHT MIND: "I am taking life seriously."

277.

WRONG MIND: "Writing is a serious undertaking and I am not a serious person. I am more of a buffoon."

RIGHT MIND: "I am taking life seriously."

278.

WRONG MIND: "I have different beliefs from most of the people I know. I shouldn't write."

RIGHT MIND: "I can't allow the beliefs of others to silence me. I will write."

279.

WRONG MIND: "It is dangerous to tell the truth about people in power. Therefore, I will not write."

RIGHT MIND: "Survival is not a small issue, but I want to expose the corrupt powers that be. I will look this hard decision right in the eye."

280.

WRONG MIND: "I live in a small community and I should only write nice, pleasant things."

RIGHT MIND: "Getting along with others is important, but so is witnessing. I may have to tell the truth and accept the consequences."

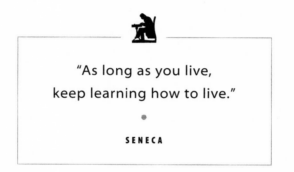

"As long as you live,
keep learning how to live."

SENECA

281.

WRONG MIND: "I want a child, not a novel. You can't have both."

RIGHT MIND: "There may be a lot to figure out, a lot to do, and a lot of luck involved, but I want both."

282.

WRONG MIND: "I want a nice home, not published poetry. You can't have both."

RIGHT MIND: "There may be a lot to figure out, a lot to do, and a lot of luck involved, but I want both."

283.

WRONG MIND: "I want a career, not a memoir. You can't have both."

RIGHT MIND: "There may be a lot to figure out, a lot to do, and a lot of luck involved, but I want both."

284.

WRONG MIND: "If I write in a dense, opaque, convoluted way, use jargon, have words mean one thing in one sentence and another thing in the next, and so on, no one—including me—will ever know that I don't have much to say and that I haven't really thought through my material."

RIGHT MIND: "I will think through my material and write clearly."

285.

WRONG MIND: "I'm sure that I can set my novel in medieval Vienna without doing any research. So what if I know nothing about medieval Vienna? Verisimilitude is overrated and no agent, editor, or reader will miss the authentic details of time, place, and setting."

RIGHT MIND: "I will research medieval Vienna and provide the necessary details of time, place, and setting."

Teaching Yourself Right Thinking

Who teaches? You do. You teach yourself. You teach at work. You teach your children. You teach when you intend to teach and you teach inadvertently, when you do a good deed or when you don't.

You teach when you stand up in front of a classroom, when you supervise, when you facilitate a meeting, and when you sit in front of your computer and start running a tutorial program. You teach when you pass along a tradition and when you break with tradition. You teach when you chat with your children as you drive, when you change your mind, and when you tell yourself something new. Who teaches? You do.

Teach yourself right thinking.

286.

WRONG MIND: "My book is no good."

RIGHT MIND: "My book is not good yet. More work is required to make it good."

287.

WRONG MIND: "I have no talent."

RIGHT MIND: "I have a head, heart, and hands—in short, I have everything I need in order to write well."

288.

WRONG MIND: "People in my position have no chance. We are always discriminated against."

RIGHT MIND: "Excellent writing is regularly produced by outcasts, pariahs, and others on the fringe. I am in fine company."

289.

WRONG MIND: "I was taught that telling the truth—about mom's drinking, about dad's anger, about Uncle Harry touching me, or about the strange customs of our religion—only got you a smack. I learned that lesson very well—all too well."

RIGHT MIND: "I am teaching myself a new lesson, that it is excellent to tell the truth."

290.

WRONG MIND: "Dan just published *another* book! May he die a horrible death!"

RIGHT MIND: "I am very sad about my low status on the publishing world totem pole, but I am not defeated."

291.

WRONG MIND: "I will write anything, just so long as it gets published."

RIGHT MIND: "I care about what I write."

292.

WRONG MIND: "I will write anything, just so long as it has a chance of making money."

RIGHT MIND: "I care about what I write."

293.

WRONG MIND: "I will write any cynical, false thing, just so long as it has a chance of becoming a bestseller."

RIGHT MIND: "I care about what I write."

Right Thinking Postulate

Given the choice between believing that you do not matter, for which you have abundant evidence, and believing that you do matter, which has the earmarks of an illusion, you are better off coming down on the side of believing that you matter.

294.

WRONG MIND: "Writing is such a romantic way to live!"

RIGHT MIND: "Writing can be a meaningful vocation."

295.

WRONG MIND: "Writing is such a bohemian career choice!"

RIGHT MIND: "Writing can be a meaningful vocation."

296.

WRONG MIND: "Writing is such a sexy thing to do!"

RIGHT MIND: "Writing can be a meaningful vocation."

297.

WRONG MIND: "Writing is too hard."

RIGHT MIND: "Writing is hard and I am a writer."

298.

WRONG MIND: "Writing pays too little."

RIGHT MIND: "Writing may pay little, but I am a writer."

299.

WRONG MIND: "The world has no need for writers."

RIGHT MIND: "The world desperately needs its writers and I am writer."

Write Mind II

Please let me know the wrong things you have been accustomed to saying to yourself and the right things you have learned to say. Your contribution may well find its way into a *Write Mind II*. I will attribute you by first name and last initial, unless you want your whole name used or unless you want to remain anonymous.

Send your contribution to me, Eric Maisel, at amaisel@sirius.com. You can also send a fax or leave a brief phone message at (925) 689-0210. If you have a moment, you might also take a peek at my websites, www.ericmaisel.com and www.sleepthinking.com

About the Author

Eric Maisel is a psychotherapist and creativity coach who works with creative and performing artists in his private practice and leads workshops for writers at writers' conferences and other venues. His twenty-two works of fiction and nonfiction include *A Life in the Arts*, *Affirmations for Artists*, *Fearless Creating*, and other books on the creative life. He teaches writing at St. Mary's College in Moraga, California, and holds a Ph.D. in counseling psychology, master's degrees in creative writing and counseling, and bachelor's degrees in psychology and philosophy. Dr. Maisel lives in Concord, California, with his wife, Ann Mathesius Maisel, and their two daughters, Natalya and Kira.